TECHNICAL REPORT

Historical Cost Growth of Completed Weapon System Programs

Mark V. Arena, Robert S. Leonard,
Sheila E. Murray, Obaid Younossi

Prepared for the United States Air Force

Approved for public release; distribution unlimited

PROJECT AIR FORCE

The research reported here was sponsored by the United States Air Force under Contract F49642-01-C-0003. Further information may be obtained from the Strategic Planning Division, Directorate of Plans, Hq USAF.

Library of Congress Cataloging-in-Publication Data

Historical cost growth of completed weapon system programs / Mark V. Arena ... [et al.].
   p. cm.
   "TR-343."
   Includes bibliographical references.
   ISBN 0-8330-3925-3 (pbk. : alk. paper)
   1. United States—Armed Forces—Procurement—Costs. 2. United States—Armed Forces—Weapons systems—Costs. I. Arena, Mark V.

UF503.H57 2006
355.6'212—dc22

2006013512

The RAND Corporation is a nonprofit research organization providing objective analysis and effective solutions that address the challenges facing the public and private sectors around the world. RAND's publications do not necessarily reflect the opinions of its research clients and sponsors.

RAND® is a registered trademark.

Published 2006 by the RAND Corporation
1776 Main Street, P.O. Box 2138, Santa Monica, CA 90407-2138
1200 South Hayes Street, Arlington, VA 22202-5050
4570 Fifth Avenue, Suite 600, Pittsburgh, PA 15213
RAND URL: http://www.rand.org/
To order RAND documents or to obtain additional information, contact
Distribution Services: Telephone: (310) 451-7002;
Fax: (310) 451-6915; Email: order@rand.org

Preface

This report is one of a series from a RAND Project AIR FORCE project, "The Cost of Future Military Aircraft: Historical Cost Estimating Relationships and Cost Reduction Initiatives." The purpose of the project is to improve the tools used to estimate the costs of future weapon systems. It focuses on how recent technical, management, and government policy changes affect cost. This report complements another document from this project, *Impossible Certainty: Cost Risk Analysis for Air Force Systems* (Arena et al., 2006), and includes a literature review of cost growth studies and a more extensive analysis of the historical cost growth in acquisition programs than appears in the companion report. It should be of interest to those involved with the acquisition of systems for the Department of Defense and to those involved in the field of cost estimation.

The research reported here was sponsored by the Principal Deputy, Office of the Assistant Secretary of the Air Force (Acquisition), Lt Gen John D. W. Corley, and conducted within the Resource Management Program of RAND Project AIR FORCE. The project's technical monitor is Jay Jordan, Technical Director of the Air Force Cost Analysis Agency.

Other RAND Project AIR FORCE reports that address military aircraft cost estimating issues include the following:

- *An Overview of Acquisition Reform Cost Savings Estimates*, in which Mark Lorell and John C. Graser (2001) used relevant literature and interviews to determine whether estimates of the efficacy of acquisition reform measures are robust enough to be of predictive value.
- *Military Airframe Acquisition Costs: The Effects of Lean Manufacturing*, in which Cynthia R. Cook and John C. Graser (2001) examined the package of new tools and techniques known as "lean production" to determine whether it would enable aircraft manufacturers to produce new weapon systems at costs below those predicted by historical cost-estimating models.
- *Military Airframe Costs: The Effects of Advanced Materials and Manufacturing Processes*, in which Obaid Younossi, Michael Kennedy, and John C. Graser (2001) examined cost-estimating methodologies and focused on military airframe materials and manufacturing processes. This report provides cost estimators with factors useful in adjusting and creating estimates based on parametric cost-estimating methods.
- *Military Jet Engine Acquisition: Technology Basics and Cost-Estimating Methodology*, in which Obaid Younossi, Mark V. Arena, Richard M. Moore, Mark A. Lorell, Joanna Mason, and John C. Graser (2003) presented a new methodology for estimating military jet engine costs; discussed the technical parameters that derive the engine de-

velopment schedule, development cost, and production costs; and presented quantitative analysis of historical data on engine development schedule and cost.

- *Test and Evaluation Trends and Costs in Aircraft and Guided Weapons*, in which Bernard Fox, Michael Boito, John C. Graser, and Obaid Younossi (2004) examined the effects of changes in the test and evaluation (T&E) process used to evaluate military aircraft and air-launched guided weapons during their development programs.
- *Software Cost Estimation and Sizing Methods: Issues and Guidelines*, in which Shari Lawrence Pfleeger, Felicia Wu, and Rosalind Lewis (2005) recommended an approach to improve the utility of software cost estimates by exposing uncertainty and reducing risks associated with developing the estimates.
- *Lessons Learned from the F/A-22 and F/A-18 E/F Development Programs*, in which Obaid Younossi, David Stem, Mark A. Lorell, and Frances M. Lussier (2005) evaluated historical cost, schedule, and technical information from the development of the F/A-22 and F/A-18 E/F programs to derive lessons for the Air Force and other services to improve the acquisition of future systems.
- *Impossible Certainty: Cost Risk Analysis for Air Force Systems*, in which Mark V. Arena, Obaid Younossi, Lionel A. Galway, Bernard Fox, John C. Graser, Jerry M. Sollinger, Felicia Wu, and Carolyn Wong (2006) described the various methods for estimating cost risk and recommended attributes of a cost risk estimation policy for the Air Force.

RAND Project AIR FORCE

RAND Project AIR FORCE (PAF), a division of the RAND Corporation, is the U.S. Air Force's federally funded research and development center for studies and analyses. PAF provides the Air Force with independent analyses of policy alternatives affecting the development, employment, combat readiness, and support of current and future aerospace forces. Research is conducted in four programs: Aerospace Force Development; Manpower, Personnel, and Training; Resource Management; and Strategy and Doctrine.

Additional information about PAF is available on our Web site at http://www.rand.org/paf.

Contents

Figures

Tables

Summary

Review of Cost Growth Literature

Overall, most of the studies we reviewed reported that actual costs were greater than estimates of baseline costs. The most common metric used to measure cost growth is the cost growth factor (CGF), which is defined as the ratio of the actual cost to the estimated costs. A CGF of less than 1.0 indicates that the estimate was higher than the actual cost—an underrun. When the CGF exceeds 1.0, the actual costs were higher than the estimate—an overrun.

Studies of the weapon system cost growth have mainly relied on data from Selected Acquisition Reports (SARs). These reports are prepared annually by all major defense acquisition program (MDAP) offices within the military services to provide the U.S. Congress with cost, schedule, and performance status. The comparison baseline (estimate) typically corresponds to a major acquisition decision milestone (e.g., Milestone II).

Prior studies have reported Milestone (MS) II CGFs for development costs ranging from 1.16 to 2.26; estimates of procurement CGFs ranging from 1.16 to 1.65; and total program CGFs ranging from 1.20 to 1.54. Regarding the differences among cost growth due to service, weapon, and time period, prior studies tended to find the following:

- Army weapon systems had higher cost growth than did weapon systems for the Air Force or Navy.
- Cost growth differs by equipment type. Several reasons are given for the differences including technical difficulty, degree of management attention, and protection from schedule stretch.
- Cost growth has declined from the 1960s and 1970s, after it was recognized as an important problem. However, improvement with recent acquisition initiatives has been mixed.

The literature describes several factors that affect cost growth. The most common ones included acquisition strategies, schedule, and others, such as increased capabilities, unrealistic estimates, and funding availability.

Analysis of Historical Acquisition Cost Growth in the Department of Defense

Our analysis also shows that, by and large, the Department of Defense (DoD) and the military departments have underestimated the cost of buying new weapon systems. (See pp. 21–24.) For our analysis, we used a very specific sample of SAR data, namely only programs that are complete or are nearly so.[1] We deliberately chose to analyze completed programs so that we could have an accurate view of the total cost growth. It typically takes many years before the complete cost growth emerges for a program. Development costs continue to grow well past the beginning of production. Previous studies have mixed both complete and ongoing programs—potentially biasing their cost growth downward. While this sample selection reduces our sample size, we think that we have a better measure of final cost growth.

Figure S.1 shows the cost growth of programs that dealt with systems that were similar to those procured by the Air Force (e.g., aircraft, missiles, electronics upgrades).[2] The metric (total CGF) displayed in the figure is the ratio of the final cost to that estimated at MS II (or its equivalent). The figure shows that the majority of programs had cost overruns.

The analysis indicates a systematic bias toward underestimating the costs and substantial uncertainty in estimating the final cost of a weapon system. Our analysis of the data indicates that the average adjusted total cost growth for a completed program was 46 percent from MS II and 16 percent from MS III. The bias toward cost growth does not disappear until about three-quarters of the way through system design, development, and production.

In contrast to the previous literature, we observed very few correlations with cost growth. (See pp. 27–38.) We observed that programs with longer duration had greater cost growth. Electronics programs tended to have lower cost growth. Although there were some

Figure S.1
Distribution of Total Cost Growth from MS II Adjusted for Procurement Quantity Changes

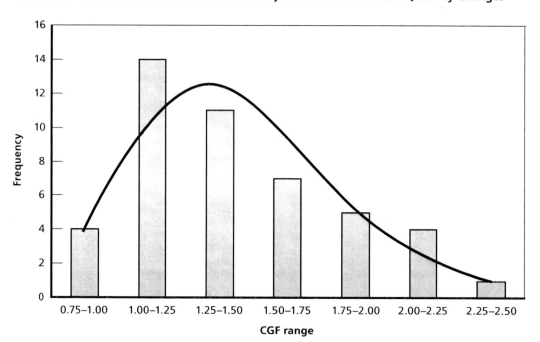

---

[1] We defined the program as complete if that program had delivered 90 percent or more of its procurement quantity or if the final SAR has been submitted.

[2] The data have been modified to mitigate the effects of inflation and changes in the number of units procured.

differences in the mean total CGF among the military departments, the differences were not statistically significant. While newer programs appear to have lower cost growth, this trend appears to be due to factors other than acquisition policies.

Abbreviations

2SLS	two-stage least squares
CBO	Congressional Budget Office
CDF	Cumulative Distribution Function
CER	cost-estimating relationship
CGF	cost growth factor
CIC	cost improvement curve
DE	development estimate
Dem/Val	demonstration and validation
DoD	Department of Defense
DSCPD	Defense System Cost Performance Database
DTC	design to cost
EMD	engineering and manufacturing development
FRP	full-rate production
FSD	full-scale development
FY	fiscal year
GAO	Government Accountability Office
IDA	Institute for Defense Analyses
IOC	initial operational capability
IOT&E	initial operational test and evaluation
ln	natural log
LRIP	low-rate initial production
MDAP	major defense acquisition program
MS	milestone
MYP	multiyear procurement
NASA	National Aeronautics and Space Administration
NAVSEA	Naval Sea Systems Command
NAVSHIPSO	NAVSEA Shipbuilding Support Office
OLS	ordinary least squares
PA&E	Program Analysis and Evaluation

PAF	Project AIR FORCE
PdE	production estimate
PE	planning estimate
SAR	Selected Acquisition Report
SDD	system design and development
SOTAS	Standoff Target Acquisition System
T1	first unit cost
T&E	test and evaluation
TPP	total package procurement
WBS	work breakdown structure

CHAPTER ONE

Introduction

Cost growth is the term used for the increase of the actual (or final) cost of acquiring a system or capability relative to the value estimated. There is a presumption in defense acquisition that the final cost is typically greater than that estimated. Our assessment of the historical record in the United States is consistent with the belief of a bias of higher actual cost relative to estimates. However, in this document, we will use the term cost growth more generally, in that growth could be positive (costs underestimated) or negative (costs overestimated).

For several decades, researchers have sought to characterize, understand, and reduce cost growth for the acquisition of military capability in the United States. Why such interest in cost growth? Cost growth is first and foremost a metric reflecting how well one estimates cost. When examining this metric over many programs, we find two important aspects: central tendency (e.g., mean value) and dispersion (e.g., variance). The central tendency indicates how well, on average, one estimates future costs. A consistent positive or negative average (bias) indicates that the estimating process could be lacking in some respect. In general, a system should seek to be neutral with respect to cost growth. That is, a system is neither systematically high nor low, on average. Dispersion is a measure of variability around that average, or, crudely, a measure of how well one does on any one particular estimate relative to the mean. A low variability, which is desirable, indicates that estimates are consistent and reflect the unique aspects of an individual program. An estimating system that is "in control" has minimal bias and low variability.

Problems with Bias and Variability in an Estimating System

Bias in an estimating system leads to financial problems for an organization. Consistent underestimation leads to poor financial planning whereby anticipated cash flow is consistently low. In the private sector, such a cash flow problem could lead to additional debt assumption or potential cancellation and loss of any sunk costs. In the weapon acquisition area, cash flow shortfalls could lead to reprogramming, other shortfalls, quantity reductions, or funding reductions for other programs. Consistent overestimation creates different problems. By overestimating, lower-priority expenditures may be eliminated that could actually fit within a given budget. Overestimating could also lead to poor cost discipline. The funds that are in excess of what is actually required might be spent on additional or improved capability that is not required (i.e., gold plating).

Bias in an estimating system can also lead to poor decisions. Having accurate cost forecasts is one criterion of proper cost-benefit analysis. If the relative costs are understated, then an organization might make investments that have a poor return. Similarly, an inconsistent bias could lead to the selection of a wrong alternative when an organization needs to choose between several options. Finally, bias in cost estimating can undermine credibility and cause decisionmakers to discount estimate information.

A high variability indicates that a system cannot forecast any specific program precisely. While on average a collection of programs might be close to budget, one could be far off the mark for any individual program. A high variability, or dispersion, in cost growth is problematic for two reasons. One reason is that high variability in cost growth makes it very difficult to choose between alternative approaches or solutions. One is unsure about the relative costs between the two alternatives. Second, if a collection of programs contains a mix of programs of different sizes (total cost), then a positive or negative growth for a large (higher dollar value) program can overwhelm the total budget. Essentially, the cash flow is dominated by one highly uncertain program.

This Study

This research is part of a broader study examining cost risk analysis for the U.S. Air Force. In the broader study, RAND is examining methods of assessing cost risk, biases introduced into the estimating process, and potential policies that could be adopted to standardize risk assessment. An analysis of cost growth fits into this broader study in that it is an empirical way to evaluate cost risk (see Appendix B for more discussion of such an approach).

The specific task of this project is to assist the Air Force in developing a cost risk policy. The bulk of the research in support of that task is described in a companion report, *Impossible Certainty: Cost Risk Analysis for Air Force Systems* (Arena et al., 2006). This report complements the companion report and provides a limited literature review of cost growth studies and a more detailed analysis of historical estimates of cost growth in Department of Defense weapon acquisition programs.

How This Report Is Organized

This report contains four chapters and three appendixes. Chapter One provides an introductory overview of the research. Chapter Two contains the results of our literature review. Chapter Three provides a methodological description of the data we used and our treatment of the data. Chapter Four presents our analysis of the data. Appendix A lists the acquisition programs we used for our data. Appendix B defines baseline estimate definitions for the RAND SAR database. Appendix C explores quantity normalization approaches.

CHAPTER TWO

Literature Review of Cost Growth Analysis

In this chapter, we review prior studies on cost growth that are readily available in the public domain. Our limited literature search included reports from research organizations, dissertations, theses, government reports, and journal articles.[1] Our objectives for this review were to compare estimates of cost growth in the acquisition of major weapon systems and summarize the findings from quantitative analyses of the factors related to cost growth.

Issue in the Measurement of Cost Growth

Before reviewing prior analyses of cost growth, this chapter provides a description of the data used to measure cost growth, how cost growth is measured, and the normalization typically applied to those measures.

Weapon System Cost Data

The primary source of data for the cost growth studies we reviewed was the Selected Acquisition Reports (SARs). SARs provide data in the form of annual reports that summarize the current program status of major defense acquisition programs (MDAPs).[2] These reports provide a high-level way to monitor cost and schedule performance of programs. According to a Department of Defense (DoD) Web site,

> SARs summarize the latest estimates of cost, schedule, and technical status. These reports are prepared annually in conjunction with the President's budget. . . . The total program cost estimates provided in the SARs include research and development, procurement, military construction, and acquisition-related operation and maintenance (except for pre-Milestone B programs which are limited to development costs pursuant to 10 USC §2432). Total program costs reflect actual costs to date as well as future anticipated costs. All estimates include anticipated inflation allowances (DoD, 2004).

---

[1] It should be noted that this literature review is not comprehensive. Many articles discuss cost growth for weapon systems (Sipple, White, and Greiner, 2004; and a 1990 unpublished draft RAND report, for example). We limited our review to those articles that we could readily find through open sources and those that reported growth factors for an aggregated sample of programs.

[2] MDAPs are programs with estimated development and procurement costs that are greater than certain threshold values. The thresholds have varied over time. Currently, they are $365 million (fiscal year [FY] 2000) for development and $2.19 billion (FY 2000) for procurement.

The SAR data, then, form one of the better ways to track cost estimates and schedules for major defense programs.

Using SAR data to study cost growth has some limitations. While these reasons have been thoroughly discussed elsewhere (Hough, 1992), it is worthwhile to summarize some of these limitations here.

- **High-Level Data.** The cost data contained in the SARs is at a high level of aggregation (e.g., development, production, and military construction, and includes costs for all contractors plus government costs), so that doing in-depth cost growth analysis (for example, at a work breakdown structure [WBS] level) is not possible.
- **Baseline Changes, Modifications, and Restructuring.** The baseline cost estimate frequently evolves or changes as the program matures and uncertainties are resolved. This shifting baseline makes the study of cost growth across programs difficult. Not all programs make similar or consistent baseline shifts and the choice of the "correct" baseline from which to measure growth is not unambiguous.
- **Reporting Guidelines and Requirement Changes.** Over the years in which SARs have been issued, thresholds and reporting guidelines have evolved. Thus, comparing data across time periods can be challenging. This problem is particularly important when looking for trends.
- **Inconsistent Allocations of Cost Variances.** The SARs allocate the difference between the baseline estimate and current estimate into one of seven variance categories: economic, quantity, estimating, engineering, schedule, support, and other. While there are guidelines on how to allocate cost growth to these categories, the actual allocation is determined by each program. These variance data are sometimes viewed as being inconsistent between programs, and, moreover, not helpful in determining the actual cause of the variance.
- **Incomplete or Partial Weapon System Cost.** Sometimes, the SAR data for a program may not comprise the total system cost. For example, the earlier ship programs separated the system and shipbuilding costs. Thus, the cost growth for such programs may be misstated by looking at only one component of the total cost.
- **Exclusion of Certain Types of Programs.** Not all programs for DoD report SARs. Those below the reporting threshold (by cost) do not have SARs. Furthermore, special access programs do not appear in the reports. Some programs received exemptions for other reasons (such as those systems acquired under "Other Transaction" authority).
- **Ambiguity of the Estimate Basis.** While the reported estimate in the SAR is the official program office position, the basis for that estimate is somewhat unclear. Do the values represent the estimate by the program office, contractor, independent group, or some combination?
- **Unidentified Risk Reserve.** Some programs include risk reserve funds to guard against cost growth. These funds are meant to cover cost increases that may happen for a variety of anticipated reasons. Because unallocated funds or allowances are ripe targets for budget cuts, risk reserve (if included) is usually buried in the estimate and not separately identified. One program might experience low cost growth relative to another because it had a greater reserve despite having similar technical and programmatic risk.

Program reports often complement SARs, especially for systems started before the advent of the SARs in 1968, and conversations with program offices regarding, for example, the explanations for changes in schedule and scope of weapon systems.

Several research organizations have used SARs to construct databases that can be used to estimate cost growth. For example, RAND developed the Defense System Cost Performance Database (DSCPD). This database contains computed cost growth measures based on SAR data. In addition, schedule information and other program information are quantified or coded and included in a spreadsheet. The Naval Sea Systems Command (NAVSEA) Shipbuilding Support Office (NAVSHIPSO) has prepared a cost growth database for the Office of the Director of Program Analysis and Evaluation. It includes data drawn from SARs for 138 systems that passed milestone (MS) II between 1970 and 1997.[3] The database also contains a classification of cost growth due to mistakes and decisions. NAVSHIPSO analysts distributed cost growth between these two categories based on the explanations in the cost variance section of the SARs.

Measuring Cost Growth

Measures of cost growth are typically presented as a ratio of the current estimate of cost to some earlier estimate of cost. The value of the ratio is strictly positive; cost overruns are greater than one while underruns are less than one. Some studies refer to this measure as a cost growth factor (CGF). Subtracting one from this ratio expresses the cost growth as a percentage of the estimated costs (see, for example, Tyson, Nelson, Om, and Palmer, 1989; Tyson, Harmon, and Utech, 1994; Drezner et al., 1993; and Sipple, White, and Greiner, 2004). In this case, positive values indicate cost overruns while negative values indicate cost underruns.

Adjustment to Cost Growth Measures

Hough (1992) and Jarvaise, Drezner, and Norton (1996) noted that in measuring cost growth, viewpoints differ regarding what to count and when to start counting. The estimates of cost growth may be reported in current or then-year dollars and without regard to changes in procurement quantity. Analysts and policymakers use unadjusted estimates to illustrate the effect of cost growth on the federal budget, regardless of the conditions responsible for cost growth. To measure the performance of program management in estimating and controlling costs, analysts typically use cost values that adjust for inflation and changes in procurement quantity. Tyson, Nelson, Om, and Palmer (1989) made a further adjustment to development cost by selecting the development cost reported by initial operational capability (IOC) as the "final" development cost. Their view was that growth beyond this point is for model changes or enhanced capability.

Although these inflation and quantity adjustments are common, the quality and consistency of SAR data have implications for analysis of costs. Hough (1992) provides a thorough discussion of these issues. We briefly summarize his points here. Cost estimates reported in SARs are adjusted by DoD for inflation. DoD inflation factors, Hough noted, are

---

[3] At milestone II, the government describes the system and makes a baseline estimate of costs and schedule called the development estimate (DE). If the system is approved, the program moves into engineering and manufacturing development.

subject to political manipulations, especially for estimates of future costs, and are crude measures that are not adjusted for regional variations in wage and prices.

Hough (1992) reported three accepted methods for adjusting for changes to the originally estimated quantity. The first method adjusts procurement costs by the amount reported in the SAR quantity variance category. The second method normalized procurement costs using cost-quantity curves. Hough described a third hybrid method:

> Procurement costs are adjusted by first deducting the amounts reported in the SAR as being quantity-related (including those amounts reported in the "Quantity" variance category, as well as those dollar amounts reported in other variance categories but identified in the narrative as quantity related) and then deducting the normalized (using cost-quantity curves) residual procurement variance (pp. 38, 40).

At the time of his study, Hough noted that the Government Accountability Office (GAO) and the Congressional Budget Office (CBO) preferred the first method, Institute for Defense Analyses (IDA) the second, and RAND the third. For reasons discussed later in this report, RAND adopted the second method in 1998. As Hough noted, when quantity has changed frequently and by a large margin, the method used can result in strikingly different values of cost growth for the same program.

An important consideration in estimating cost growth is deciding from which point to measure the difference between the actual or current estimate and a baseline estimate of costs. The defense acquisition process uses a "gated" system, in which approvals are given to proceed to the next phase along with a commitment to funding at a specific milestone point. The system has evolved since its initial implementation such that the names for the milestones have changed (i.e., MS I, II, III versus MS A, B, C).[4] We will use the older nomenclature for milestones throughout the document, as the majority of programs analyzed were completed under the older system. (In fact, most of the cost growth literature designates the milestones using the older system.)

Costs are estimated and updated several times in the acquisition process. For each milestone, there is, theoretically, a baseline estimate: planning, development, and production estimates. The planning estimate (PE) occurs at the time of the MS I[5] (now identified as MS A), usually at the award of a concept exploration/concept development or demonstration and validation contract. The development estimate (DE) occurs at the time of MS II[6] (the closest analogous milestone currently is MS B), usually at the award of a system design and development (SDD) contract.[7] In the cost growth literature, the DE is the most common baseline used. The production estimate (PdE) occurs at the time of MS IIIA, MS IIIB, or simply MS III[8] (the closest analogous milestone currently is MS C), usually at the award of the low-rate initial production (LRIP) or full-rate production (FRP) contract.

---

[4] A full discussion of the current and former acquisition process is beyond the scope of this document. Those readers interested in a more complete description should review the *Defense Acquisition Guidebook* (Defense Acquisition University, 2004).

[5] MS I is the approval to enter into Phase I, Program Definition and Risk Reduction.

[6] MS II is the approval to enter into Phase II, system design and development.

[7] Other names used in the past for the major development effort in MDAPs are engineering and manufacturing development (EMD) and full-scale development (FSD).

[8] MS III is the approval to enter into Phase III, Production or Fielding/Deployment.

The recorded MS points for the RAND SAR database, however, do not always correspond to particular PE, DE, or PdE baselines. In some cases, baselines were never formally established. In other cases, the declaration of the baseline occurred after a significant contract award. In all cases, the SAR estimate that was designated as a particular baseline estimate (e.g., MS I, MS II, MS III) was the one that best represented the state of information regarding the program at the time the milestone-related *contract* was awarded. In most cases, there are no differences between the milestone and contract award. However, these milestone dates were occasionally modified so that all programs represented a similar point of *financial commitment*. Appendix B details these definitions.

The SARs show budgeted costs for the currently approved quantity. RAND and IDA typically normalize the current estimate to the quantity associated with the baseline estimate (e.g., PE, DE, or PdE). As Hough (1992) points out, the baseline from which cost growth factors are estimated using this method does not change if subsequent quantities change.

Estimates of Cost Growth and Factors Affecting Cost Growth

In this section, we present estimates of cost growth from the studies using historical data. Table 2.1 describes the data sources, time period, and sample used for estimating cost growth. Estimates for cost growth for development, procurement, and total program costs are given. Unless noted, all cost growth measures are adjusted for inflation and quantity from an MS II baseline. Also included in the table are the results for the analysis that is described in Chapter Four.

Almost all of the studies used the most recent December SAR for the current estimate or the last SAR for the "actual" cost.[9] For studies before the advent of SARs, researchers gathered costs and related data from concept papers, historical memoranda, and weapon system reports. McNicol (2004) used the database NAVSHIPSO developed for Program Analysis and Evaluation (PA&E) using SAR data. The only two studies in this overview that do not use SARs are Wandland and Wickman (1993), and Tyson, Nelson, and Utech (1992). Wandland and Wickman considered weapon system contracts managed at Wright Aeronautical Laboratories and four product centers in the Air Force Materiel Command (Aeronautical Systems Center, Electronics Systems Center, Space Systems Center, and Armament Systems Center). Tyson, Nelson, and Utech considered cost growth for National Aeronautics and Space Administration (NASA) programs.

Wide ranges of time periods were explored, although most considered time periods that spanned at least 10 years. The number of weapon systems included in a cost growth analysis ranged from six missile programs (Shaw, 1982) to 138 weapon systems (Tyson, Nelson, Om, and Palmer, 1989).

Studies reported cost growth one of two ways: percentage change or the ratio of actual to planned costs (also called a growth factor). For consistency of presentation, we convert percentage change estimates to growth factors in Table 2.1. All studies reported positive average (or mean) cost growth. Some individual weapon systems had cost underruns (see, for

---

[9] Note that by SAR reporting convention, the last SAR does not correspond to the final cost, as the last SAR occurs before the end of the program. SAR reporting ends when a program reaches 90 percent of either the estimated cost or the procurement quantity. However, the costs for the final SAR should be very close to the final cost, as most of the funding has been spent at that point.

example, Shaw, 1982; and McNicol, 2004). Estimates of average CGFs for development costs range from a low of 1.16 for the nine ship weapon systems reviewed in Asher and Maggelet (1984) to a high of 2.26 for six missile programs studied in Shaw (1982). Estimates of procurement cost growth ranges from a low of 1.24 for 12 aircraft systems to a high of 1.65 for the 89 weapon systems built between 1960 and 1987 that were reviewed by Tyson, Nelson, Om, and Palmer (1989). Total program costs ranged from a high of 1.54 for 20 tactical missiles developed and built between 1962 and 1992 (Tyson, Harmon, and Utech, 1994) to a low of 1.20 for 120 weapon systems from 1960 to 1990 (Drezner et al., 1993).

Shaw (1982) reported a wide range of growth factors across the six missile systems. Two systems (AIM-7M and AIM-9M) had no cost growth in development costs, while development costs for the AIM-7F and the AIM-9L programs grew by over 300 percent. Total unit procurement cost growth factors were less varied, ranging from 1.10 for the AIM-7E/E2 to 1.9 for the AIM-9L.

Tyson, Nelson, and Utech (1992) considered cost growth for 23 space programs with cost and program size information. They found that actual total costs for space programs were 101 percent higher than planned. When weighted for program size, total cost growth was slightly higher (total CGF of 2.10 compared with 2.01).

Estimates of cost growth are much higher in the years prior to the early attempts to reduce acquisition costs through the Packard Initiatives. For example, an unpublished 1959 draft RAND report estimated total cost growth for 24 weapon systems acquired between 1946 and 1959. It reported an unadjusted total cost growth factor of 6.06 and a growth factor adjusted for inflation and quantity of 3.23 for these systems.

McNicol (2004) considered the distribution of procurement cost growth from mistakes (defined as unrealistic cost estimates or poor management) and found that cost growth was skewed to low or negative cost growth. Almost 70 percent of systems (96 out of 138) experienced procurement cost growth (from mistakes) between −20 and 30 percent (or a CGF between 0.8 and 1.30) and seven programs experienced growth less than −20 percent (or a growth factor less than 0.8). Thirty-five systems in the sample had a mistake component of procurement cost growth of at least 30 percent (a CGF of 1.30). These findings are not reported in the table.

Table 2.1
Cost Growth Measures

Citation	Data Sources	Time Period	Sample	Reported Measure	CGFs		
					Development	Procurement (Production)	Total Program
Tyson, Nelson, Om, and Palmer (1989); Wolf (1990)	SARs (last SAR for program or December 1987) and concept papers	1960–1987	89 weapon systems	Mean ratio	1.27 (n = 80)	1.65 (n = 63)	1.51 (n = 63)
Tyson, Harmon, and Utech (1994)	SARs (last SAR for program or December 1992) and historical memoranda	1962–1992	20 tactical missiles / 7 tactical aircraft	Median ratio / Mean ratio	1.26 (n = 20) / 1.20 (n = 7)	1.59 (n = 20) / 1.17 (n = 7)	1.54 (n = 20) / 1.20 (n = 7)
McNicol (2004)	PA&E database	1970–1997	138 that passed MS II and had completed at least 3 years EMD and had not entered acquisition process at MS IIIa or MS IIIb	Average percentage change from DE baseline	1.45 (n = 138)	1.28 (n = 138)	Not reported
Drezner et al. (1993)	SARs (last SAR for program or December 1990 SAR)	1960–1990	128 programs with DE	Average adjusted CGF n	1.25 (n = 115)	1.18 (n = 120)	1.20 (n = 120)
Unpublished 1959 draft RAND report	Weapon system reports	1946–1959	24 weapon systems (9 fighters, 3 bombers, 4 cargos/tanks, 8 missiles)	Adjusted total factor increase	Not reported	Not reported	3.23 (n = 24) (st. dev. 2.273)
				Unadjusted total factor increase	Not reported	Not reported	6.06 (n = 24) (st. dev. 5.4)
Shaw (1982)	Last SAR for program or latest available	1973–1982	6 intercept missile programs	Percentage change in development cost growth and unit total cost procurement growth (FSD to procurement) for each weapon system	2.26 (n = 6)	1.43 (n = 6)	Not reported
Asher and Maggelet (1984)	Last SAR for program or December 1983	As of December 1983	52 systems that had achieved IOC	DE to IOC; mean cumulative total development CGF; cumulative total procurement unit cost growth factor at IOC	1.52 (n = 52)	1.30 (n = 52)	Not reported

Table 2.1—continued

Citation	Data Sources	Time Period	Sample	Reported Measure	CGFs		
					Development	Procurement (Production)	Total Program
Wandland and Wickman (1993)	Program management system contracts for 5 Air Force organizations compiled in Acquisition Management Information Systems	1980–1990	261 competed and 251 sole-source contracts	Average total CGF competed contracts Average total CGF sole-source contracts			1.14 (n = 261) 1.24 (n = 251)
Tyson, Nelson, and Utech (1992)	Marshall Space Flight Center's NASA cost model, GAO reports, related IDA projects, and NASA briefings	Not given Not given	23 space programs with cost growth and program size information 23 space programs with cost growth and program size information	Average cost growth Weighted (program size) average cost growth			2.01 (n = 23) 2.10 (n = 23)
This study (2006)	Last SAR for program	1968–2003	68 completed programs, similar complexity to those acquired by U.S. Air Force	Average cost growth (mean)	1.58 (n = 46)	1.44 (n = 44)	1.46 (n = 46)

Basic Differences in Cost Growth

Many of the studies we reviewed explored the differences among cost growth estimates across services, weapon system types, and time. We present the expected differences and report on the findings below.

Services

Differences among the services might be expected because of the difference in management styles between the services, the size (in total inflation adjusted dollars) of the programs, types of weapon systems, and the relative ages (how many years past the date of the reference baseline) of the programs. Drezner et al. (1993) found that mean total cost growth is higher in Army and Air Force weapon systems than in Navy systems.[10] Only a small part of the difference is due to the smaller size of Army programs and lower ages of the programs. Comparing cost growth attributed to mistakes in 131 weapon programs, McNicol (2004) found that Army programs exhibited statistically significantly higher procurement cost growth than did Navy programs, about 0.20 points.

Weapon System Type

Several studies compared cost growth among weapon systems. These differences would arise because some weapon systems may have more technical difficulty, which is associated with high cost growth. Also potentially contributing to these differences are organizational architectures of acquisition bureaucracies dedicated to specific weapon system types. Drezner et al. (1993) found that aircraft, electronics, and munitions have similar total cost growth. Helicopters and vehicles have higher total cost growth than the average in their sample of 120 weighted (by program size) programs,[11] while ships tend to have lower-than-average cost growth. Tyson, Nelson, Om, and Palmer (1989) found that, among the 89 programs they reviewed, tactical munitions (both surface- and air-launched) had higher procurement cost growth than did aircraft, helicopters, satellites, and strategic missiles. Tyson, Harmon, and Utech (1994) compared 20 tactical aircraft programs and 20 munitions programs and found that the maximum total CGF for tactical aircraft programs was 1.40, versus 2.23 for the tactical missile programs. Tyson, Harmon, and Utech suggest that aircraft programs receive more management attention and protection from schedule stretch than do tactical missile programs. Tyson, Harmon, and Utech also found that the highest procurement growth among aircraft was 1.42. They attributed this to technical changes made late in the program.

Time Trends

Several studies investigated whether cost growth has improved since weapon system cost growth was recognized as a problem and policymakers have tried to improve cost perfor-

---

[10] Analysis at RAND revealed that SAR-reported baselines for several Navy ship programs were not established until after one or more ships had a significant amount of construction completed. By that time, the system's costs were much better understood than they were for other programs. Hence, ship programs have low cost growth compared with the "official" baseline. See Appendix C for a discussion on SAR reporting differences for ships.

[11] Drezner et al. (1993) included 128 programs in the data sample, of which 120 could be analyzed and five were helicopter programs.

mance. Tyson, Nelson, Om, and Palmer (1989) calculated average development, production, and total production cost growth over five time intervals (early 1960s, early 1970s, late 1970s, entire 1970s, and 1980s) based on the start of full-scale development (FSD). They found that all three measures of cost growth were the highest in the 1960s. Cost growth fell in the years immediately following Packard Initiatives, increased in the late 1970s, and subsequently fell again in the 1980s. Drezner et al. (1993) also found that cost growth had not steadily improved between the 1960s and the late 1980s.

Using data on 131 weapon systems prepared by the NAVSHIPSO, McNicol (2004) found that procurement cost growth from mistakes (management decisions or unrealistic estimates) declined after 1973, when independent costing was introduced. However, development cost growth from mistakes increased in the years after 1973. McNicol suggested that independent costing techniques are better suited to estimating procurement costs.

Looking across studies in this review, we find that estimates of cost growth are much higher in the years prior to the publication of the Packard Initiatives in 1969 and other major acquisition initiatives. For example, an unpublished 1959 RAND draft report estimated cost growth for 24 weapon systems acquired between 1946 and 1959. It reported an *unadjusted* procurement CGF of 6.06 and an *adjusted* factor (adjusted for inflation and quantity) of 3.23.

Factors Affecting Cost Growth

Several studies used program information in the SARs to identify factors that potentially affect cost growth in weapon systems. These were some of the most common factors:

- Acquisition strategies: prototyping, modifications, multiyear procurement (MYP), competition in production, design to cost, total package procurement, fixed-price development, contract incentives in development, contract incentives in production
- Schedule factors: program duration, concurrency, and schedule slip
- Other factors: increased system capabilities, unrealistic cost estimates, budget trends, and management behavior.

Studies employed different methodologies to examine the impact of these factors including simple comparisons of mean CGFs, graphical analysis, statistical modeling, and reviews of program histories. Of course, authors do not always have consistent definitions of factors. For example, both the Tyson, Nelson, Om, and Palmer (1989) and Drezner et al. (1993) studies examined the effect of prototyping. However, each study used a different definition of what constituted prototyping on a program. Tyson, Nelson, Om, and Palmer (1989, p. VII-1) defined a prototype as a "working model to demonstrate specific design or operational objectives in advanced development (but not in concept exploration)—e.g., before full scale development (FSD) (Milestone II). . . ." Drezner et al.'s (1993) definition was much more expansive and included considerations for precedent systems. Thus, differences in results between studies might arise due to definition or interpretation of factors and not conflicting data.

Acquisition Strategies

In an analysis of the 128 programs that had a DE between 1960 and 1990, Drezner et al. (1993) found that programs that included prototyping had higher average total cost growth than programs without prototyping. This result was in contrast to Tyson, Nelson, Om, and Palmer (1989) finding that prototyping holds down development and procurement costs because of the knowledge gained through prototyping. Specifically, they found that development cost growth was 17 percent lower in programs with prototyping, procurement cost growth 26 percent lower, and total program cost growth 19 percent lower.[12] These differences were statistically significant in regression models that were not weighted for program size. Using dollar weights, Tyson et al. also found that programs that were prototyped exhibited statistically significant lower cost growth in development, production, and total program. As stated previously, the difference in results between Drezner et al. and Tyson, Nelson, Om, and Palmer might be due to the authors' definition of prototyping.

McNicol (2004) investigated the effect of previous experience with a weapon type or technology or of precedent systems on cost growth due to mistakes.[13] That study found that the nine systems with few relevant precedents had procurement CGFs 0.46 points higher than systems with useful precedents had. This difference was statistically significant.

Drezner et al. (1993) considered other acquisition strategies, including modifications, concurrence, and joint programs. The study found that programs that are modifications (in which case there are more accurate, initial estimates) have less total cost growth than programs starting from an all-new design.

Concurrency refers to the overlap between completion of development and the start of production. There are conflicting views about how concurrency might affect cost growth. According to Drezner et al. (1993), conventional wisdom holds that because concurrent programs move to procurement without completing development tests, a greater potential exists for cost growth. On the other hand, since the program duration is shorter, one might also expect lower cost growth (or at least lower cost). Drezner et al. investigated the relationship between concurrency and cost growth by plotting a measure of concurrency (the overlap between the completion of initial operational test and evaluation [IOT&E] and the beginning of low-rate production) versus cost growth. Looking only at concurrent programs, they found that programs with higher concurrency have lower total cost growth. Drezner et al. are cautious not to dismiss conventional wisdom: A detailed examination of a few programs indicated that, in some cases, the dates of IOT&E completion and the beginning of low-rate production were not representative of actual events.

Drezner et al. (1993) hypothesized that management complexity, through the establishment of joint programs, would present coordination challenges that would increase cost growth. However, they found that the total cost growth was lower for joint programs than for single-service programs.

---

[12] The estimated coefficients of the prototype indicators in the regressions to predict development, production, and total program cost growth ratios were –0.25, –0.466, and –0.298, respectively. The sample size was 36 weapon programs.

[13] McNicol does not define how programs were classified by whether there were precedents. The nine programs with few relevant prototypes were the UH-60A Blackhawk helicopter (1972), the CH-53 Super Stallion/MH-53 Sea Dragon helicopters (1975), AH-64 Apache helicopter (1976), the CH-47 Chinook helicopter (1978), the M1 Abrams tank (1976), the Bradley Fighting Vehicle System (1978), the M712 CLGP Cannon-Launched Guided Projectile (1975), the CBU-97B Sensor Fused Weapon (1985), and the Sense-and-Destroy Armor 155-mm projectile (1988). Drezner et al. (1993) classified a program as having a precedent if there was previous experience with this system type or technology.

Tyson, Nelson, Om, and Palmer (1989) used separate regression analysis to estimate the effectiveness of several acquisition initiatives on development, procurement, and total program cost growth by equipment types: aircraft, tactical munitions, and other (electronics/avionics, strategic missiles, and satellites). They found mixed evidence of these initiatives. The study only reported statistically significant differences.

In terms of development cost growth, Tyson, Nelson, Om, and Palmer (1989) found that programs with fixed-price development had higher cost growth factors than programs without fixed-price development, a difference of 0.28 points. Programs with contract incentive in FSD did not consistently display lower cost growth. Aircraft and tactical munitions displayed no difference in development cost growth with incentives where other program types (e.g., electronics, missiles, satellites) did show lower development cost growth.

In terms of total cost growth, the study reports that all programs with total package procurement (TPP) had higher growth than programs without TPP, a difference of 0.42 points. Only the "other" program types had lower cost growth with contract incentives in FSD, a difference of 0.65 points.

McNicol (2004) also considered the effect of acquisition strategies. That study found that programs negotiated through TPP also exhibited statistically significant higher procurement CGFs (0.44 points) than programs without TPP for the "mistakes" portion of procurement cost growth.

Comparing mean cost growth measures, Tyson, Nelson, Om, and Palmer (1989) found that procurement cost growth is 0.31 points lower for approved MYP programs than for non-MYP programs; total program cost growth is 0.24 points lower. They investigated whether program stability rather than MYP was responsible for the lower cost growth. To do this, they compared the cost growth of the MYP programs to otherwise "stable" programs (defined as candidate MYP programs that had been rejected by Congress for MYP or were only recently approved for MYP funding). They found that approved MYP programs had lower procurement and total program cost growth ratios than rejected MYP programs had, a difference of 0.07 and 0.06 points, respectively.[14] Although the differences in the sample means suggest that MYP lowers cost growth, the study could not find a statistically significant relationship using regression analysis between MYP and cost growth measures.

Tyson, Nelson, Om, and Palmer (1989) also considered the effect of competition and design on cost by comparing mean cost growth measures for programs with and without these features. In terms of competition, the study found that cost growth (total and procurement) was higher for competitive programs than for all other programs. However, considering only tactical munition programs (where competition is more likely), cost growth is lower for competitive programs.

In terms of design to cost (DTC), the study found that the total cost growth ratio in the DTC programs is 0.19 points greater than that of the non-DTC programs. However, Tyson et al. point out that DTC programs of the late 1970s were more successful, as the total cost growth ratios of those DTC programs were 0.35 points lower than non-DTC programs of the same era.

---

[14] The sample of candidate MYP programs excludes the Improved Hawk program because it was a continued modification program that is not typical of the major acquisition programs in their overall sample.

Schedule Factors

Drezner et al. (1993) plotted the time from MS I to IOC against total CGF to examine the effect of the length of the program. The study found that longer programs have higher cost growth. Tyson, Nelson, Om, and Palmer (1989) estimated a regression model to predict total program cost growth. That study found that development schedule growth, program stretch, and development schedule length are associated with higher total cost growth.

Drezner et al. (1993) plotted total cost growth and months of slip in the first operational delivery to explore the effect of schedule slip on cost growth. They found no relationship.

Tyson, Harmon, and Utech (1994) used two-stage least squares (2SLS) and ordinary least squares (OLS) models to predict the effect of schedule changes on cost growth of tactical missile programs. The 2SLS model controls for a simultaneous relationship between cost growth and schedule growth. The estimates from the 2SLS model suggest that, all else equal, for tactical missiles a one-point (100 percent) increase in development schedule growth would increase development cost growth by 0.38 points. Estimates from OLS models, which do not control for the influence of cost growth on schedule growth, suggest positive correlations as well: A one-point increase in procurement stretch is associated with a 0.29-point increase in procurement cost growth, and a one-point increase in schedule growth is associated with a 0.37-point increase in total procurement cost growth. For tactical aircraft, the study found that schedule growth variables are positively related to cost growth. Tyson, Harmon, and Utech noted that inference from the small sample (seven programs) was not reliable.

Bielecki (2003) estimated a logistic regression model to estimate the effect of schedule, estimating, support, and other changes on development cost overruns. This study found that schedule growth was correlated with cost growth.

Other Factors

McNicol (2004) proposed three mechanisms that may cause cost growth. The mechanisms include (1) a decision to increase the capabilities of the system beyond what was approved and captured in procurement estimates; (2) an unrealistic estimate of procurement cost; (3) poor program execution or exceptional budget instability.

McNicol explored the evidence for the first mechanism by reviewing the program history and cost growth trends for programs with extreme cost growth (35 systems; see McNicol, 2004, Table 14, p. 81) to determine if the cost growth was associated with a change in what was procured. The program histories revealed that 14 of these systems had substantial changes in what was procured. For two of these systems (the Bradley and Stand-off Target Acquisition System [SOTAS]), McNicol concluded that these changes were "unforced"—that is, they were not adopted to meet the MS II requirements, but rather were enhancements to procure a more capable system. McNicol suggested that the growth for the remaining systems was also "unforced" as well, primarily because these programs did not make extensive use of advanced technologies where forced cost growth might be expected to meet the requirements.

For 15 of the programs with extreme procurement cost growth, McNicol's review of program history suggested that unrealistic estimates of procurement costs (the second mechanism) were made. McNicol explored this possibility in his regression analysis of the mistake components of 131 weapon systems. McNicol suggests that the services have a propensity toward optimistic costing (with higher cost growth for Army programs). However, the statistical model did not support a competing theory of overly optimistic estimates related to budget "tightness." According to McNicol (and also Drezner et al., 1993), this theory posits that, in times of tight budgets, an optimistic estimate is put forth and thus one would see higher cost growth. This theory was not supported by McNicol's regression results: Systems put in place during tight budgets exhibited less cost growth. Similarly, Drezner et al. (1993) looked at trends in budgets (annual change in proposed total obligation authority) and average cost growth; they also found that in times of increasing budgets, cost growth increases, and that as budgets decline, cost growth also declines.

Finally, McNicol explored the evidence on his proposed third mechanism. From his regression analysis, McNicol concluded that budget instability and changes in acquisition management structure adopted in the late 1980s that relaxed management oversight were statistically associated with higher procurement growth. However, in his review of the program histories of systems with extreme cost growth, these mechanisms did not seem to be present.

Summary

In this chapter, we summarized cost growth literature for the acquisition of major weapon systems. Overall, most studies reported overall positive cost growth. Estimates of adjusted average CGFs for development costs range from 1.16 to 2.26; estimates of procurement cost growth ranged from 1.16 to 1.65; and total program CGFs ranged from 1.20 to 1.54.

We reported the finding of studies regarding the differences among cost growth due to service, weapon, and time period. Studies tended to find the following:

- Army weapon systems had higher cost growth than did weapon systems for the Air Force or Navy.
- Cost growth differs by equipment type. Several reasons are given for the differences including technical difficulty, degree of management attention, and protection from schedule stretch.
- Cost growth improved from the 1960s and 1970s after cost growth was recognized as an important problem. However, improvement with acquisition initiatives since then has been mixed.

The literature describes several factors that affect cost growth. The most common factors included acquisition strategies, schedule, and other factors such as increased capabilities, unrealistic estimates, and budget trends.

There was mixed evidence of the effectiveness of acquisition strategies. One study demonstrated that increased system capabilities due to decisions outside of the control of program managers increased program costs. However, that same study could not rule out the adoption of unrealistic estimates as a source of cost growth.

CHAPTER THREE

Data for Analysis of Cost Growth in DoD Acquisition Programs

This chapter describes the data we used to analyze historical cost growth in DoD, the sample size, the metric we used to characterize that growth, and how we normalized the data so we could draw meaningful comparisons across acquisition programs that spanned a considerable time period.

Cost Growth Data

As described in the previous chapter, over the last several years, RAND has collected and organized SAR cost data to serve as a basis for understanding and characterizing cost growth. Currently, the data collected by RAND is organized into a database comprised of about 220 programs based on SAR information from 1968 through 2003.[1] The database mainly focuses on cost, schedule, quantity, and categorical[2] data from the SARs.

Research Approach

The SAR data have been an invaluable tool for cost research and have been used for several studies done by RAND and others in the cost analysis field. Many of these studies focused on some aspects of weapon system cost growth, such as characterizing growth, examining trends, and looking for factors that correlate with cost growth.

Sample Selection

For this analysis, we have used a subset of information in the RAND SAR database. We used multiple screening criteria for select programs for the sample. First, we selected a subset of programs that were similar in type to those procured by the Air Force (e.g., aircraft, missiles, electronics upgrades) and excluded those that were not (e.g., ships). From these programs, we selected programs that have finished (defined as >90 percent production complete). Thus, we excluded almost all of the 81 ongoing programs, plus all those canceled prior to initiation of FRP. This criterion was used to make certain we could determine the "true" or "actual" final costs and not some projection. In the remaining programs, we analyzed each MS baseline to

---

[1] The current dataset consists of 220 of the approximately 300 programs with SARs. RAND has not completed normalization analysis for 80 Army and Navy programs that ceased SAR reporting 10 or more years ago, so these programs are not included in the current database.

[2] These data include lead service, contractor, system type, and aspects of the development strategy.

ensure that it represented the point in time at which the program committed to that program phase. If no estimate was available at or near the time of the commitment to the relevant program phase, then the program's cost growth from that baseline was excluded from the dataset. The resulting dataset included 68 programs. In Appendix A, we list the programs selected.

The selection of completed programs is different from the approach taken in other studies of cost growth that were outlined in the previous chapter. Most of the other studies included a mix of complete and ongoing programs in their analysis. We have deliberately chosen to exclude ongoing programs from this analysis. Our view is that the inclusion of ongoing programs biases cost growth estimates, because it takes considerable time for the actual cost growth to emerge for a program. In the subsequent analysis, we will show that, indeed, only late in a program does the full cost growth typically emerge.

Cost Growth Metric

As our metric for cost growth, we chose the cost growth factor (CGF). The metric is the ratio of final costs to baseline estimated costs. We present CGFs measured from either MS II or MS III estimates.[3] Values less than zero are not possible. To have a negative CGF would imply the government was paid to acquire a system—clearly not a realistic situation. Given the discontinuity at zero, one might expect that the statistical distributions of CGF would be non-normal. We explore the form of the CGF distribution as part of this research.

Normalization

In this study, we adjust for inflation and changes in the quantity produced. We use the original base-year cost values reported in the SARs. Thus, CGFs have changes due to inflation largely removed.[4]

To remove the effects of quantity changes, we adjusted all the SAR production cost estimates to the final quantity produced. The adjustment uses a cumulative average cost improvement curve (CIC) (improvement slope and first unit cost [T1] values) derived from annual funding data provided in each program's SAR. If the production quantity reported in the baseline estimate SAR was less than that in the final, we calculated the estimated cost of units not built and added that to the baseline estimate. Similarly, if the production quantity reported in the baseline SAR was more than that in the final estimate, we calculated the estimated cost of the additional units and subtracted that from the baseline estimate.[5]

This quantity adjustment is different from the approaches used by others in that we normalize to the final quantity and not the quantity of a particular baseline estimate. This approach has a couple of advantages:

1. The one value we care most about, the actual cost, is not changed. In other words, all estimates are adjusted and the actual costs are left unmodified.

---

[3] Note that the milestones differ for the current acquisition system. However, as we are using historical data, we retain the milestone names defined at the time of the programs.

[4] Admittedly, it is quite difficult to make perfect adjustments for inflation or to create general escalation indices that represent multiple programs' unique situations. Nonetheless, calculations using base-year values should largely remove the major effects of inflation.

[5] We have made no correction for rate of production, which also can be affected when quantity is changed.

2. The weighting of the procurement cost as part of the total costs reflects the weighting of that actually spent. For example, suppose the production quantities were cut dramatically. Adjusting the procurement costs to the final quantity would reduce the relative importance of the procurement growth in calculating the total cost growth. If the other adjustment method were used (adjusting the final procurement cost to the estimated quantities), the total CGF would be weighted more strongly by the procurement cost growth.

In Appendix C, we explore the differences in quantity normalization on the overall results. The results are not substantially different using different normalization methods.

Because annual funding includes resources for both the current year's units and advanced procurement for future years' units, and because annual funding is a mixture of recurring and nonrecurring costs, the use of annual funding data to define CICs is open to interpretation. We interpreted these data to best reflect the cost of units built at the end of the production run, because that is the portion of the CIC in which our adjustment is made.

We present values for unadjusted quantity as well. The unadjusted CGFs are useful in that they represent the "funding" uncertainty. The quantity-adjusted CGFs are more representative of the "estimate" uncertainty (see Drezner et al., 1993).

The SARs also report causes of cost growth in other categories (e.g., economic, schedule, engineering) in the "variance analysis" section. Aside from inflation and quantity adjustments, we have made no further normalizations.

CHAPTER FOUR

Cost Growth Analysis

In this chapter, we characterize CGF for the SAR data in several ways. We segment the data by funding category, milestone, and commodity type to accommodate different approaches. For most of the data, we display simple summary statistics. In the second half of this chapter, we present significant data correlations and trends.

Segment CGF Results

Funding Category

The SAR cost data are broken out into the following categories:

- Development
- Procurement
- Military Construction
- Operations and Maintenance (acquisition related)
- Total Cost.

Very few MDAPs include acquisition-related operations and maintenance funding. A larger number, but still a small fraction, of all MDAPs include military construction funding. As a result, we do not analyze these categories separately but do include their funding (if any) in the Total Cost category. As described in the previous chapter, we calculate two CGFs for procurement: one adjusted and another unadjusted for quantity changes. As a result, we will also display two CGFs for Total Cost—adjusted and unadjusted for quantity. Table 4.1 shows the summary statistics for each category using MS II SAR estimates as the baseline.

Table 4.1
CGF Summary Statistics by Funding Categories for MS II

Category	Number of Observations	Mean	Median	Standard Deviation	Minimum	Maximum
Total (adjusted)	46	1.46	1.44	0.38	0.77	2.30
Total (unadjusted)	46	1.65	1.25	1.08	0.37	5.56
Development	46	1.58	1.34	0.79	0.77	5.47
Procurement (adjusted)	44	1.44	1.40	0.42	0.51	2.29
Procurement (unadjusted)	44	1.73	1.30	1.37	0.28	7.28
Military construction	10	1.33	1.11	0.82	0.51	2.87

The statistics in Table 4.1 raise some interesting points. The first observation is that there does seem to be a consistent underestimation of cost (a bias in estimating). Both the mean and median for each of the categories are well above 1.0. Another observation is that the distributions are skewed. This can be noted from the fact that the mean is consistently higher than the median. Another point to note is the decrease for the mean, standard deviation, and minimum and maximum range when comparing the adjusted procurement and total numbers to the unadjusted ones. On average, procurement quantities grew by approximately 30 percent for the sample—hence the larger values for the unadjusted growth.

The shape of the CGF distribution allows us to gauge the magnitude of the variability and hence the approximate uncertainty of estimates. Figure 4.1 shows the distribution of the total CGF for quantity-adjusted growth with MS II as the baseline. The bars on the chart represent the actual frequency distribution of the data sample. The solid line is a lognormal fit to the data using the mean and standard deviation of the sample in log space: 0.34 and 0.26, respectively. Note that the lognormal distribution is a fairly good, but not perfect, fit. The actual distribution seems to be a bit more peaked and has a slightly flatter tail than the fitted distribution. However, these differences from the ideal fit could be due to the small sample size of 46 observations.

Figure 4.1
Distribution of Total Cost Growth from MS II Adjusted for Procurement Quantity Changes

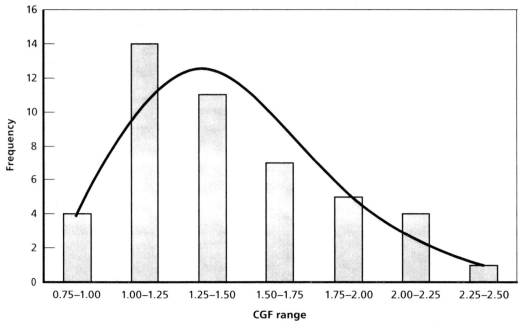

RAND TR343-4.1

Compared to previous studies, we find higher cost growth. For example, Figure 4.1 shows that for almost 70 percent of our sample, total CGFs were 1.25 or higher. Considering a larger sample of weapon systems, McNicol (2004) found that about 40 percent of his sample had a procurement CGF greater than 1.30.[1]

Table 4.2 displays the summary statistics for each of the categories using MS III SAR estimates as the baseline. The general trends are similar to those for MS II, but the CGFs are lower and have less variability than the MS II values—as one might expect for a more mature point in the program. If one point is dropped from the Military Construction mean and standard deviation, values change quite significantly. An important observation is that development costs continue to grow from MS III. When examining individual program annual funding data, it appears that this growth is likely due to requirements growth, model changes, or technical update or refresh.

Similar to the studies reviewed in Chapter Two, the development CGF tends to be higher than adjusted procurement CGFs. The development CGF estimates fall within the range of estimates from previous studies (1.16 to 2.26). Procurement and total CGF estimates also are within the bounds of the literature (1.16, 1.65) and (1.20, 1.54), respectively. However, this study tends to find higher cost growth than did past studies.

We explored the source of these differences by comparing our estimates to another RAND study that used the RAND dataset. Drezner et al. (1993) also reported CGFs for a similar breakdown. Table 4.3 compares the means for CGFs at MS II reported by this study and by the 1993 study. Note that it was not possible to compare all the categories in Tables 4.1 and 4.2, as the 1993 study did not report them.

Table 4.2
CGF Summary Statistics by Funding Categories for MS III

Category	Number of Observations	Mean	Median	Standard Deviation	Minimum	Maximum
Total (adjusted)	68	1.16	1.13	0.26	0.48	2.30
Total (unadjusted)	68	1.25	1.04	0.79	0.31	5.01
Development	65	1.30	1.10	0.64	0.89	5.47
Procurement (adjusted)	68	1.19	1.17	0.33	0.29	2.52
Procurement (unadjusted)	69	1.27	1.01	1.06	0.01	6.36
Military construction	26	5.26[a]	0.77	22.31[a]	0.11	117[a]

[a] One high growth observation (value 117) significantly skews the mean higher. Without this observation, the mean is 0.81 and the standard deviation is 0.51.

---

[1] To explore the shape of the distribution further, we used the Box-Cox method to determine a transformation that normalizes the data (Box and Cox, 1964; and Stata Corporation, 2003, pp. 128–137). The method determines the best value for the parameter λ for the transform given in this equation:

$$y' = \frac{y^{\lambda} - 1}{\lambda}.$$

When λ is 1.0, the distribution is essentially unchanged (already close to normal). A lognormal transformation results when $\lambda = 0$. A reciprocal transformation results when $\lambda = -1$. Applying this method to MS II CGF for total cost, $\lambda = 0.21$. The transformation is close to a lognormal one but not exact. $\lambda = 0.24$ for the total CGF for an MS III baseline.

Table 4.3
A Comparison of the CGF Means for MS II Between This Study and the RAND 1993 Study

Category	Current Study	1993 Study
Total (adjusted)	1.46	1.30
Development	1.58	1.25
Procurement (adjusted)	1.44	1.18
Procurement (unadjusted)	1.73	—

An almost consistent increase of about 0.20 occurs between the 1993 study and this one. These results do not imply that the previous analysis is in error. The baseline data and quantity adjustment factors were nearly the same. However, there were a few important differences. The quantity adjustment procedures for the 1993 study differ somewhat from the ones used here. The 1993 study used the cost variance data reported in the SARs to adjust for quantity changes. For this analysis, we adjust the procurement cost using cost improvement curves as described above. Perhaps the most significant difference lies in the sample of programs. The early study included all programs in the database at least three years past EMD, whereas this one selected only completed programs. This difference certainly suggests that including only completed programs is necessary to reflect final CGFs. We have also excluded a few types of programs from the analysis (e.g., ships), which could contribute to the difference.

Milestone

One might expect that, as a program passes through successive milestones, the mean of the CGFs should tend toward 1.0 and the standard deviation should decrease. In other words, the estimates should become more accurate and precise as the program matures. Indeed, these trends appear in the data. Table 4.4 shows the CGF for adjusted total cost by milestone, and Table 4.5 shows the unadjusted values.

Table 4.4
CGF for Adjusted Total Cost by Milestone

Milestone	Mean	Standard Deviation	Number of Observations
MS I	1.46	0.50	5
MS II	1.45	0.36	43
MS II/III	1.59	0.65	3
MS III	1.14	0.21	67

Table 4.5
CGF for Unadjusted Total Cost by Milestone

Milestone	Mean	Standard Deviation	Number of Observations
MS I	1.86	1.20	5
MS II	1.60	0.98	43
MS II/III	2.33	2.32	3
MS III	1.20	0.65	67

Note that there is a combined MS II/III category for programs that passed both milestones in a single year. These programs had simultaneous contractual commitments for major development and initial production (not a production option).[2] Given the small number of observations for the MS I and the combined MS II/III, it is difficult to make a definitive statement on the progression between all the milestones. Yet, a clear progression occurs in both mean and standard deviation between MS II and MS III.

How do estimates improve in between the milestones? As SARs are collected on an annual basis, we can track trends in cost growth at more points than just the milestones. However, programs have quite different durations. The durations between the MS II and final SARs ranged from 4 years to over 25 years. To normalize the different durations, we examined the cost growth as the fraction of time between MS II and the program end. To weight programs evenly, we broke the time into 11 uniform segments (i.e., 0 percent, 10 percent, 20 percent, . . . , 100 percent). When there was not an exact match between the SAR available and the interval, we used linear interpolation to estimate the value. Figure 4.2 shows a box plot for total adjusted CGF for each 10 percent time interval, where 1.0 is the last SAR of the program and 0 is the MS II SAR. (The points in the graph are the observations that fall outside of the box and whisker range.)

Figure 4.2
Total Adjusted CGF Box Plots by Fraction of Time Between MS II and Final SAR

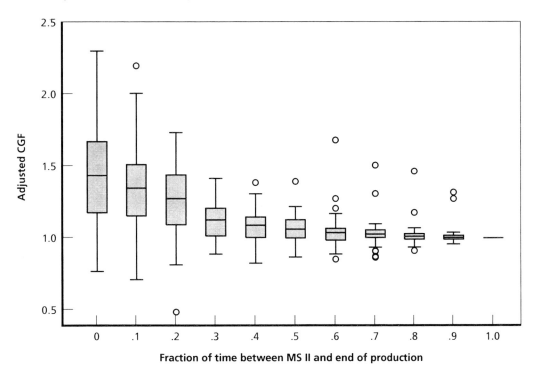

Fraction of time between MS II and end of production

RAND *TR343-4.2*

---

[2] Many major development contracts include an option for initial production. For these programs, the MS III is specified as the date that option is exercised, if it indeed is.

As can be observed from the figure, the CGF tends toward 1.0 and the variability decreases as the program matures. Not until the 70 to 80 percent point does the CGF average 1.0. That is, on average, the estimate is the same as the final cost (no bias).

Commodity Types

In the process of collecting SAR cost data, RAND segregated the programs by the type of system being produced. Table 4.6 lists and provides examples of the commodity categories in the data sample. Table 4.7 shows the CGFs for adjusted total cost by each commodity category.

Clearly, differences occur between CGFs for the various commodities. Given the limited number of observations for each category, it is difficult to say whether the differences are statistically meaningful. As we will see in the next section, the electronic programs do tend to have lower cost growth that is statistically significant. The previous literature has also found differences between weapon types. For example, Tyson, Nelson, Om, and Palmer (1989) and Tyson, Harmon, and Utech (1994) found that aircraft have lower cost growth than missile systems. Drezner et al. (1993) also found that vehicles tended to have higher cost growth than other systems.

Table 4.6
Acquisition Commodity Categories

Commodity	Program Example
Aircraft	A-10, B-1B, F-16
Cruise missiles	AGM-129A (ACM), B/R/UGM-109 (Tomahawk)
Electronic aircraft	E-2C, E-3A (AWACS), EF-111A
Electronics	B-1B CMUP-Computer, FAAD C2I, SMART-T
Helicopters	C/MH-53D/E, OH-58D (AHIP)
Launch vehicles	IUS, Titan IV (CELV)
Missiles	AGM-65A/B (Maverick), AIM-54C (Phoenix)
Other	CSRL, MK-60 (Captor)
Satellites	DMSP, GPS Sat BlkI/II/IIA
Vehicles	M-2A3 (Bradley upgrade)

Table 4.7
CGF for Adjusted Total Cost by Commodity Class for MS II

Commodity	Mean	Standard Deviation	Number of Observations
Aircraft	1.35	0.24	9
Cruise missiles	1.64	0.40	4
Electronic aircraft	1.52	0.47	5
Electronics	1.23	0.33	12
Helicopters	1.76	0.21	3
Launch vehicles	2.30	N/A	1
Missiles	1.52	0.38	8
Other	1.40	N/A	1
Satellites	1.55	0.57	2
Vehicles	1.67	N/A	1

Correlations and Trends

In the first part of this chapter, we explored descriptive statistics for CGFs segregated in different ways. This section will explore correlations and trends of the CGFs. We caution the reader that the correlations are *associative* and not *causal*. Thus, a significant correlation does not imply that a certain factor or characteristic *causes* cost growth. Rather, such a relationship indicates a propensity or likelihood of having a higher or lower cost growth. This qualification has important consequences when considering an acquisition policy. As we will see, programs that have longer development and production durations tend to have higher total cost growth. An unfounded policy implication would be to shorten all programs to lower cost growth. In fact, such a policy might have the opposite effect, as programs might need to be accelerated beyond an efficient pace. The actual cause of such a relationship, as has been discussed, could be due to causes such as the need to update and refresh obsolete technology or a change in requirements due to external reasons (e.g., war, change in administration, funding constraints).

Another consideration is which factors to consider when examining trends and correlation. Much of the cost-estimating relationship (CER) literature uses historical data that have been supplemented with information not included in the SARs. In this analysis, we have selected factors that can be objectively assessed or determined with limited information about the program, i.e., data or information that is readily available in a SAR or that a cost estimator could reasonably know at an early stage of the project.

Some researchers have used subjective factors (e.g., technical scales) when examining cost growth (Biery, Hudak, and Gupta, 1994). While such analyses have proven insightful, the evaluation of such factors typically requires some judgment by the analyst. Such factors can also be difficult to determine early in a program or subject to differences depending on an analyst's interpretation. Furthermore, such evaluations and correlations are done after the fact (once the program is complete) and thus have the benefit of hindsight. Again, our focus is analysis that can be objectively done.

We explored correlations of development, procurement, and total cost growth with different factors. We only report correlations where there is a statistically significant difference (5 percent chance of accepting the null hypothesis). In several cases, there are differences between means of certain populations that are not significant due either to few observations or to a large variability. Also, we will examine trends and differences in log space given the skewed nature of the distributions of the CGFs.

Development

Table 4.8 summarizes the correlations explored for development cost growth. We observed three statistically significant correlations: a trend with time (Year of MS), a difference between commodity types, and a trend with duration. The first correlation is one in which the development cost growth decreases as the year of the MS II increases. The trend is only significant if the Titan IV program (which had the highest development cost growth in the sample) is removed. Figure 4.3 shows a plot of the development cost growth versus the year of MS II.

Table 4.8
Correlations with Development Cost Growth

Factor	MS II	MS III
Service	No	No
Year of MS	Yes[a]	No
Total program cost ($)	No	No
Development cost ($)	No	No
Number of development units	No	No
Commodity type	Yes	Yes[a]
Duration between MS and program completion	Yes	Yes

[a] Subject to influential observation.

Figure 4.3
Trend of Development Cost Growth with Time

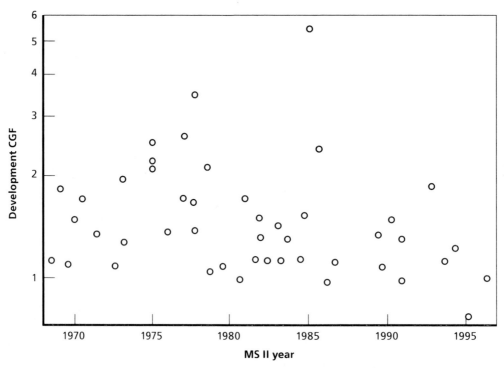

RAND *TR343-4.3*

Interestingly, the same correlation does not appear for the MS III development CGFs. While there is a trend downward with time, it is not statistically significant. The difference in observed correlation between the MS II and MS III could be due to many reasons. One possibility is that there are different causes of growth between MS II and MS III. Most of the initial research and development costs are known (actual costs) by MS III. This fact contrasts with the case for MS II where the development cost is an estimate.

The second significant correlation is that electronics programs tend to have lower development cost growth from MS II than other weapon system types. Similar to the correlation with time, the MS III development cost growth does not show the same trend. The natural log (ln) of the average development CGF (ln[CGF]) for electronics programs is 0.17

compared with the rest of the programs in the sample with a corresponding ln(CGF) of 0.45. Space programs (launch vehicles and satellites) also had significantly higher development cost growth from MS II than did other weapon system types. However, this difference was driven by one of the programs in this category: Titan IV.

The last statistically significant development cost correlation is with program duration. By duration, we mean the number of years between the milestone year and the project end (the year of the final SAR). Figures 4.4 and 4.5 show these trends for MS II and MS III, respectively. These trends suggest that longer programs have greater cost growth. There are many potential explanations for this trend, including longer programs being subject to more revisions, upgrades, and possible obsolescence issues.

Procurement

Table 4.9 summarizes the correlations explored for procurement cost growth adjusted for quantity changes. There are very few significant correlations with procurement cost growth. Similar to development, electronics programs have lower cost growth, at least for MS II. The ln(CGF) for electronics programs is 0.11 versus 0.38 for the rest of the sample. There is also a trend of higher procurement CGFs for programs with longer times between MS II and the final SAR (program end). Figure 4.6 shows the plot of the procurement CGF versus the duration between MS II and the final SAR.

Figure 4.4
Development CGF Versus Number of Years Between MS II and Final SAR

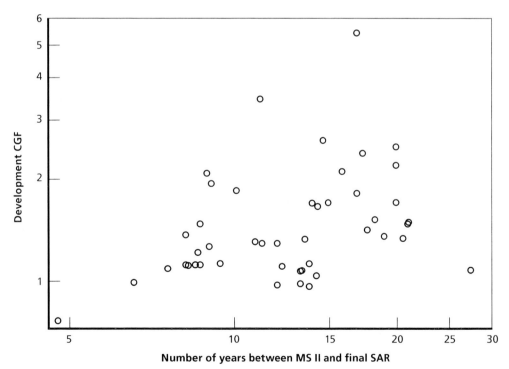

Figure 4.5
Development CGF Versus Number of Years Between MS III and Final SAR

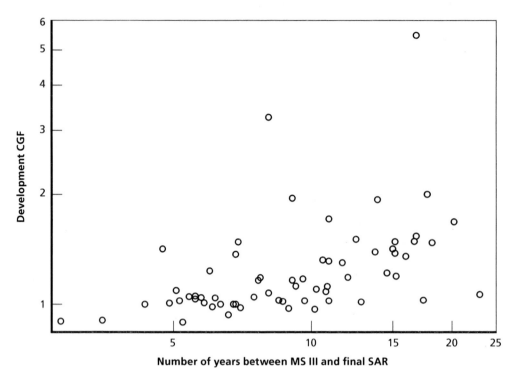

RAND *TR343-4.5*

Table 4.9
Correlations with Procurement Cost Growth Adjusted for Quantity Changes

Factor	MS II	MS III
Service	No	No
Year of MS	No	No
Total program cost ($)	No	No
Procurement cost ($)	No	No
Number of production units	No	No
Commodity type	Yes	No
Duration between MS and program completion	Yes	No

Figure 4.6
Procurement CGF (Adjusted) Versus Number of Years Between MS II and Final SAR

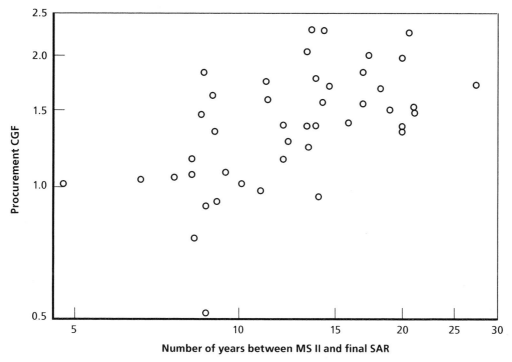

RAND *TR343-4.6*

The trends for the CGFs for unadjusted procurement largely follow the same trends as the adjusted ones with one exception. There is a trend to lower procurement CGFs with time for the MS III data. This trend results from a steady decline in quantity growth. In fact, recent programs are more likely to have quantity reductions (partially as a measure of cost control.) Figure 4.7 shows the quantity growth factor plotted versus time for MS III.

Figure 4.7
Procurement Quantity Growth Versus Time

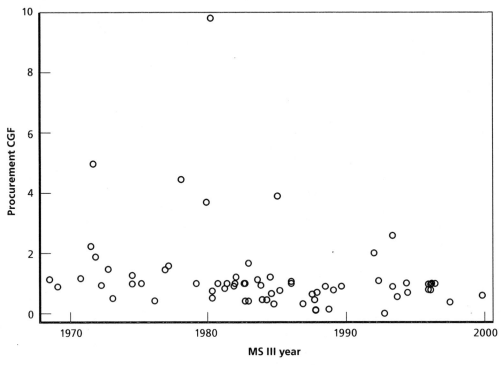

Total Cost

Table 4.10 lists the significant correlations with total cost growth (adjusted for quantity). The correlations for total cost growth follow a similar pattern to those for development and procurement. For the MS II growth, there is a slight downward trend with time (shown in Figure 4.8).

Table 4.10
Correlations with Total Cost Growth Adjusted for Quantity Changes

Factor	MS II	MS III
Service	No	No
Year of MS	Yes	No
Total program cost ($)	No	No
Ratio of development cost ($)/total program cost ($)	No	No
Ratio of procurement cost ($)/total program cost ($)	No	No
Number of production units	No	No
Number of prime firms	No	No
Commodity type	Yes	No
Duration between MS and program completion	Yes	Yes

Figure 4.8
Adjusted Total Cost Growth Versus Year of MS II

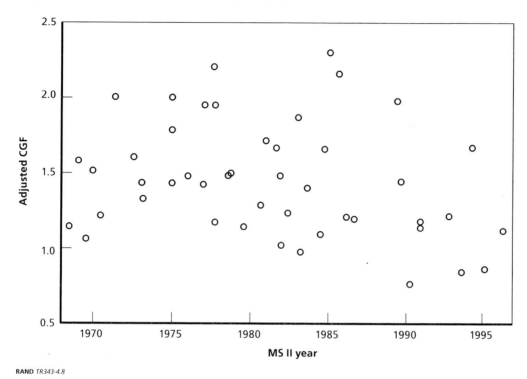

RAND TR343-4.8

However, the trend shown in Figure 4.8 could be related to the observed correlation with duration. For the more recent programs, their durations tend to be much shorter than the rest of the sample. For example, programs starting in the mid-1990s could not have a duration of more than 10 years if the program is finished (a criterion for inclusion in the analysis). Therefore, it is *not* possible to conclude that there has been improvement in total cost growth. Table 4.11 shows the average program duration by decade for the data sample. Note that the programs passing MS II in the 1990s have a much shorter average duration. Figures 4.9 and 4.10 show the correlation of adjusted total cost growth with duration between the MS and final SAR.

Table 4.11
Duration Between MS II and Final SAR by Decade

Decade	Number of Observations	Average Duration (years)
1960s	3	10.9
1970s	18	15.5
1980s	17	13.8
1990s	8	8.9

Figure 4.9
Adjusted Total Cost Growth Versus Duration Between MS II and Final SAR

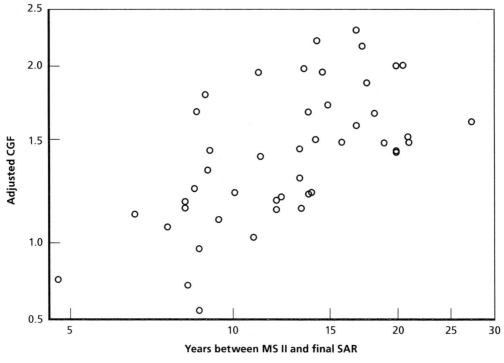

RAND *TR343-4.9*

Electronics programs, again, show a tendency toward lower cost growth. The electronics programs at MS II had an average ln(CGF) of 0.17 compared with 0.40 for the rest of the sample. For MS III, the trend was driven by one program, so we do not report a significant correlation.

**Figure 4.10
Adjusted Total Cost Growth Versus Duration Between MS III and Final SAR**

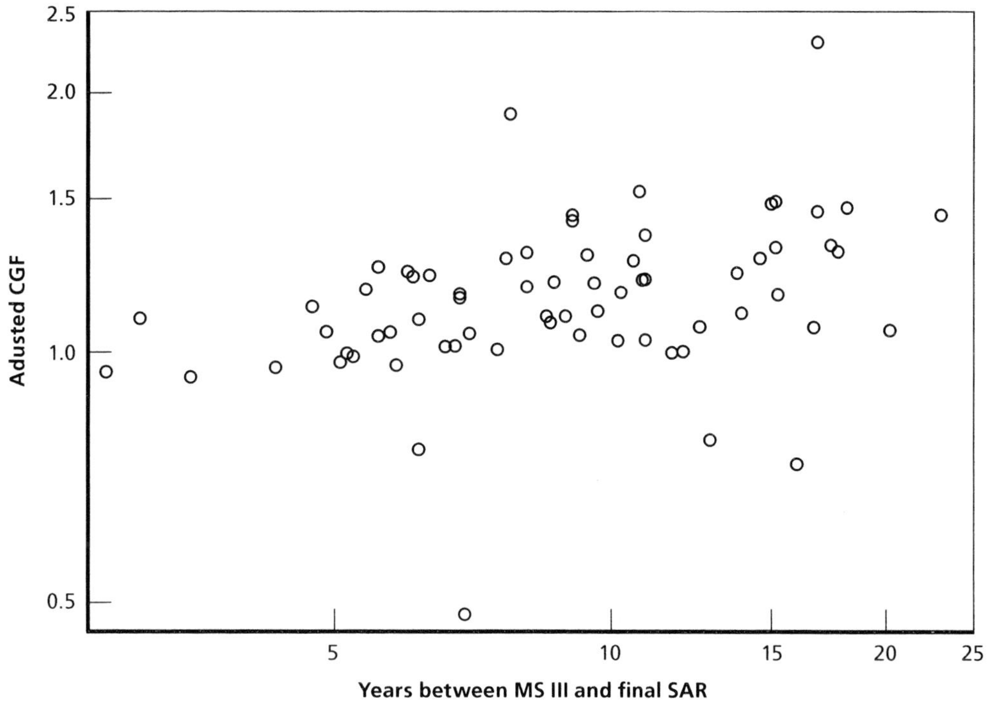

RAND TR343-4.10

Other Correlations

One other correlation is the relationship between development and procurement cost growth. One could hypothesize that there may be a correlation (either negative or positive) between the two. In other words, if cost grew in development, it will grow in production. Conversely, if cost grew in development, there should be less growth in procurement as the potential problems are resolved. Figure 4.11 shows the procurement CGF (adjusted for quantity) versus the development CGF for MS II. There is no significant correlation between the two factors. The correlation factor between the two CGFs is 0.27. Ignoring the one point with a development CGF greater than 5.0, which is highly leveraging, a regression analysis indicates an insignificant correlation ($t = 1.6$).

Figure 4.11
Development CGF Versus Adjusted Procurement CGF

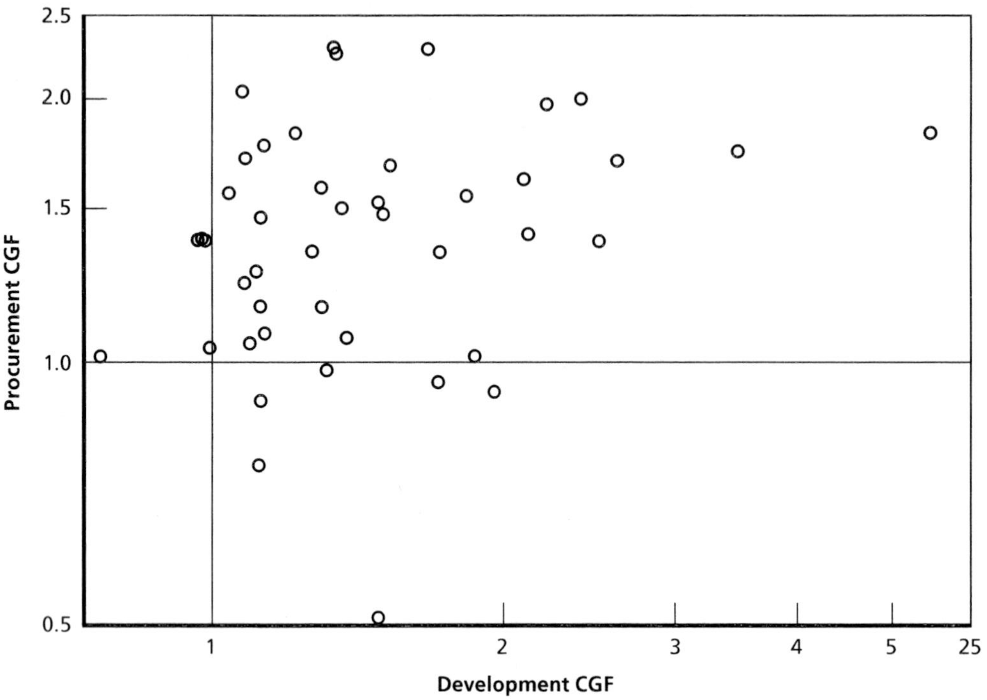

Comparison with Findings from Literature Review

Other studies have also found that older programs have higher cost growth, but cost growth has not steadily declined. For example, Tyson, Nelson, Om, and Palmer (1989) and Drezner et al. (1993) find that development, production, and total cost growth measures were highest in the 1960s, fell in the early 1970s, increased in the late 1970s, and fell again in the 1980s.

Drezner et al. (1993) also found that program length as measured by time from milestone I to IOC is associated with higher total program cost growth. Similarly, Tyson, Nelson, Om, and Palmer (1989) found that development schedule growth, program stretch, and development schedule length are associated with higher total program cost growth.

In contrast to our findings, studies we reviewed also found that cost growth differed by service type and program size. For example, Drezner et al. (1993) found that mean total cost growth is higher in Army and Air Force weapon systems than in Navy systems. McNicol (2004) also found that Army programs exhibited statistically significant higher cost growth than Navy programs. One possible explanation for these differences is that we omitted both ships and submarines from our dataset; these system types were included in both of the earlier studies. Studies have also found that larger programs (in terms of overall budget) had lower cost growth (see, e.g., Drezner et al., 1993; and McNicol, 2004). Interestingly, our sample did not show the same correlation with program size. Figure 4.12 shows a plot of the total CGF (adjusted for quantity) versus the estimated program cost for MS II. While there does not seem to be a trend with cost growth and program size, the variability does appear to be higher for the smaller programs. However, given the smaller number of large programs, one cannot be conclusive. Figure 4.13 shows a plot of the total cost growth versus the actual program cost for MS II. Note that there is not a correlation with the actual cost, either.

Figure 4.12
Adjusted Total CGF for MS II Versus Program Size (Estimated Total Cost)

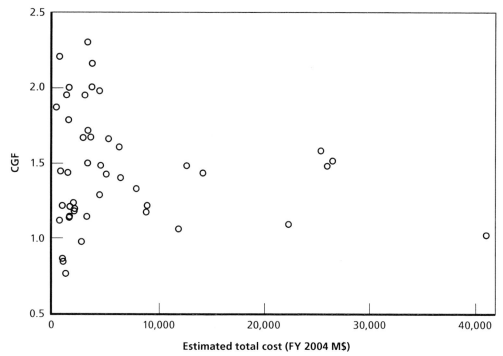

Figure 4.13
Adjusted Total CGF for MS II Versus Program Size (Actual Total Cost)

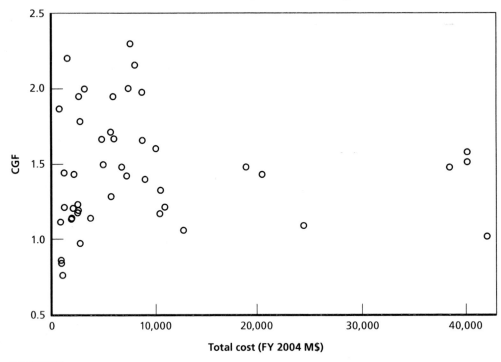

CHAPTER FIVE

Summary Observations

Using the SAR data that RAND has collected over several years, we have characterized the cost growth for major acquisition programs. We have observed the following:

- Average adjusted total cost growth for the completed program is 46 percent from MS II and 16 percent from MS III.
- This analysis shows about a 20 percent higher growth than the previous RAND SAR study. We attribute this increase to using only completed programs in the current analysis. As we demonstrate, cost growth continues for both development and production well past MS III—likely due to requirements changes and system upgrades. Another contributing factor to our higher CGF may be the sample selection (e.g., excluding ship programs).
- Cost growth bias does not disappear until three-quarters of the way through system design, development, and production. At this point, the system is well understood and a solid estimating basis is available. Further, requirements changes or upgrades slow.

We observed very few correlations with cost growth. We observed that programs with longer duration had greater cost growth. Electronics programs tended to have lower cost growth. We found no statistically significant differences between the three services. It is also difficult to say whether there has been any improvement in cost growth over time. The data do show an improving trend with time. However, our data for recent programs are biased toward ones with shorter duration, and programs that take less time to complete tend to have lower cost growth. So, we cannot say whether the trend is due to improvement or sample selection. We did observe that quantity growth tends to be decreasing. In other words, more recent trends are toward reducing quantities procured and not increasing them.

Acquisition Programs Selected

Table A.1 lists the various programs that were included in the analysis. For each program, an X indicates that some cost data were available for a particular milestone.

Table A.1
Programs Included in the Analysis by Milestone

Program Name	MS I	MS II	MS III
A-10		X	X
A-7D			X
AAQ-11/12 (LANTIRN)		X	X
AFATDS		X	X
AGM-129A (ACM)			X
AGM-65A/B (Maverick)		X	X
AGM-65D (Maverick)		X	X
AGM-86B (ALCM)		X	X
AGM-88 (HARM)		X	X
AGM/RGM/UGM-84A (HARPOON/SLAM)		X	X
AIM-120A (AMRAAM)		X	X
AIM-54C (Phoenix)		X	X
AV-8B			X
AV-8B Remanufacture			X
B-1B		X	X
B-1B CMUP-Computer		X	X
B-1B CMUP-JDAM		X	X
B-2A Spirit			X
B/R/UGM-109 (Tomahawk)		X	X
BGM-109G (GLCM)		X	X
C-5B			X
C/MH-53D/E	X	X	X
CSRL			X
DMSP			X
DSCS III		X	X
DSP			X
E-2C			X
E-3A (AWACS)	X	X	X
E-3A (AWACS) RSIP		X	X
E-4 (AABNCP NEACP)		X	X
E-6A (TACAMO)		X	X

Table A.1—Continued

Program Name	MS I	MS II	MS III
E-8A (JSTARS)		X	X
EF-111A		X	X
F-5E			X
F-14A		X	X
F-14D Tomcat		X	X
F-15		X	X
F-16		X	X
F/A-18		X	X
FAAD C2I	X	X	X
FAADS LOS-R (Avenger)			X
GPS Sat BlkI/II/IIA		X	X
IUS			X
JSIPS			X
JSTARS-CGS	X	X	X
JSTARS-GSM		X	X
JTIDS Class II TDMA		X	X
Javelin (AAWS-M)		X	X
KC-135 Re-engine			X
LGM-118A (Peacekeeper)			X
Longbow Apache-FCR		X	X
Longbow Hellfire		X	X
M-1A2 (Abrams)			X
M-2A3 (Bradley upgrade)		X	X
MGM-140A (ATACMS--Block I - APAM)		X	X
MILSTAR Satellites			X
MILSTAR Terminals			X
Minuteman III			X
MK-50 (TORPEDO)		X	X
MK-60 (Captor)			X
OH-58D (AHIP)		X	X
OTH-B		X	X
S-3A		X	X
SINCGARS-V			X
SMART-T		X	X
T-45 Training System	X	X	X
Titan IV (CELV)		X	X
TRI-TAC CNCE			X
UH-60A/L		X	X
UHF Follow-On			X

Designation of Selected Acquisition Report Milestones

To keep consistency across different program types, and to mitigate the effects of changes to the acquisition system and potential rebaselining of a program, the RAND Corporation has developed the following milestone definitions. Contract award dates are the primary determinative event to designate the dates of milestone baselines. When applying the following rules, keep in mind that the overall goal of milestone baseline determination is consistency of the estimate designation date with the date that the government commits to spending the funds for that program phase. For the most part, these definitions are generally consistent with the baselines published in the SARs.

The following rules apply to all system types except ships and submarines:

- The MS I (demonstration and validation [Dem/Val] or equivalent) contract award date defines the MS I baseline. If no such effort is undertaken in the program—that is, the program begins with an FSD or EMD contract award—then no MS I baseline is designated for the program.
- The MS II or IIA (FSD/EMD or equivalent) contract award date defines the MS II baseline. In the event that multiple developmental contracts are awarded in the program, the first contract of relatively significant value determines the MS II baseline date. The contract section of the SARs provides contract value information. If no such effort is undertaken in the program (i.e., the program begins with a production contract award), then no MS II baseline is designated for the program. This usually occurs if the program is a follow-on procurement of an existing weapon system or if the program is for the procurement of a substantially off-the-shelf product.
- The MS IIIA (LRIP or equivalent) or MS III (FRP or equivalent) contract award date defines the MS III baseline. MS IIIA is the preferred date for the MS III baseline, but the actual commitment to production is defined by the relative magnitude of the value of the contract award, and the continuity of production stemming from that award date. If the LRIP contract is of small relative value, and there is a break in production following it before FRP is authorized, then the MS III date is preferred for the MS III baseline.

For ships and submarines, MS I and the MS I baseline are at the completion of the baseline or preliminary design. MS II and the MS II baseline are at the award date for the lead ship's construction. MS III and the MS III baseline are at the award date for the follow-on production contract or the start of construction for the second ship when the initial contract value included more than the lead ship.

In the absence of milestones and contract award dates in a program, acquisition program baselines or other official baselines identified in the SAR can be used as the databases' baseline(s). The program's annual expenditures track, as well as the name given to the baseline in the SAR, should be analyzed to determine whether a baseline represents MS I, II, or III. In the absence of development funding, no MS I or II is designated for the program.

An Exploration of Different Quantity Normalization Baselines

As discussed in Chapters Two and Three, there are several approaches to quantity normalization in analyzing cost growth. For the analysis presented in Chapter Four, we normalized CGF to the *final* production quantity (i.e., the quantity specified in the final SAR). This approach differed from prior practice (e.g., Drezner et al., 1993), where the normalization quantity was chosen at some milestone. However, others have noted (Hough, 1992) that the quantity normalization method can lead to different results for the calculated CGF. The question arises as to how much our calculated cost growth factors would change if we used the more traditional approach in normalizing to a milestone quantity rather than the final quantity. In this appendix, we will examine the aggregate, total CGFs normalized to the baseline quantity.

For the same set of programs used for the analysis in Chapter Four, we adjusted the final procurement cost to the quantity stated for a particular SAR and recalculated both the procurement and total CGFs. Thus, for each SAR, we calculated a quantity-corrected final cost. Table C.1 lists the procurement CGF statistics and Table C.2 lists the total CGF. Shown in each table are the unadjusted values, the values adjusted to final quantity (same method used in Chapter Four), and the values adjusted to the MS II quantity.

Table C.1
Procurement CGF Summary Statistics by Different Quantity Normalizations for MS II

Total Cost Growth	Number of Observations	Mean	Median	Standard Deviation	Minimum	Maximum
Unadjusted	44	1.73	1.29	1.37	0.28	7.28
Adjusted to final quantity	44	1.44	1.40	0.42	0.51	2.29
Adjusted to MS II quantity	44	1.42	1.40	0.39	0.39	2.27

Table C.2
Total CGF Summary Statistics by Different Quantity Normalizations for MS II

Total Cost Growth	Number of Observations	Mean	Median	Standard Deviation	Minimum	Maximum
Unadjusted	46	1.65	1.25	1.08	0.37	5.56
Adjusted to final quantity	46	1.46	1.44	0.38	0.77	2.30
Adjusted to MS II quantity	46	1.44	1.42	0.39	0.83	2.74

In terms of averages, there is very little difference between the values for either adjustment method. Thus, the results in Chapter Four are not subject to the quantity adjustment method. It should be noted that for a few programs, there are significant differences between the CGF due to the methods. These programs tend to have very large quantity changes or large shifts in cost improvement.[1] However, there are very few of these programs and they do not skew the larger sample average (correlation coefficient of 0.92 for total CGF and 0.97 for procurement cost growth).

---

[1] When tracking the course of cost growth over time for a specific program, normalizing to the original quantity results in a consistent base value and the sequence of CGFs is comparable.

References

Arena, Mark V., Obaid Younossi, Lionel A. Galway, Bernard Fox, John C. Graser, Jerry M. Sollinger, Felicia Wu, and Carolyn Wong, *Impossible Certainty: Cost Risk Analysis for Air Force Systems*, Santa Monica, Calif.: RAND Corporation, MG-415-AF, 2006.

Asher, N. J., and T. F. Maggelet, *On Estimating the Cost Growth of Weapon Systems*, Institute for Defense Analyses, IDA Paper P-1494, September 1984.

Bielecki, John V., *Estimating Engineering and Manufacturing Development Cost Risk Using Logistic and Multiple Regression*, thesis, Wright Patterson Air Force Base, Ohio: Air Force Institute of Technology, 2003.

Biery, F., D. Hudak, and S. Gupta, "Improving Cost Risk Analysis," *Journal of Cost Analysis*, 1994, pp. 57–86.

Box, G. E. P., and D. R. Cox, "An Analysis of Transformations," *Journal of the Royal Statistical Society, Series B (Methodological)*, Vol. 26, No. 2, 1964, pp. 211–252.

Coleman, Richard L., Jessica R. Summerville, and Megan E. Dameron, "The Relationship Between Cost Growth and Schedule Growth," *Acquisition Review Quarterly*, Spring 2003, pp. 117–123. Online at http://www.dau.mil/pubs/arq/2003arq/Spring2003/ColemanSP3.pdf as of February 9, 2006.

Cook, Cynthia R., and John C. Graser, *Military Airframe Acquisition Costs: The Effects of Lean Manufacturing*, Santa Monica, Calif.: RAND Corporation, MR-1325-AF, 2001. Online at http://www.rand.org/pubs/monograph_reports/MR1325/ as of February 8, 2006.

Defense Acquisition University, *Defense Acquisition Guidebook*, Version 1.0, October 17, 2004. Online at http://akss.dau.mil/dag/welcome.asp as of February 8, 2006.

DoD. See U.S. Department of Defense.

Drezner, Jeffrey A., Jeanne M. Jarvaise, Ronald Wayne Hess, Paul G. Hough, and D. Norton, *An Analysis of Weapon System Cost Growth*, Santa Monica, Calif.: RAND Corporation, MR-291-AF, 1993. Online at http://www.rand.org/pubs/monograph_reports/MR291/ as of February 8, 2006.

Fisher, G. H., *Cost Considerations in Systems Analysis*, New York: American Elseview Publishing Company, Inc., 1971.

Fox, Bernard, Michael Boito, John C. Graser, and Obaid Younossi, *Test and Evaluation Trends and Costs for Aircraft and Guided Weapons*, Santa Monica, Calif.: RAND Corporation, MG-109-AF, 2004. Online at http://www.rand.org/pubs/monographs/MG109/index.html as of February 8, 2006.

Hough, Paul G., *Pitfalls in Calculating Cost Growth from Selected Acquisition Reports*, Santa Monica, Calif.: RAND Corporation, N-3136-AF, 1992. Online at http://www.rand.org/pubs/notes/N3136/ as of February 8, 2006.

Jarvaise, Jeanne M., Jeffrey A. Drezner, and Daniel M. Norton, *The Defense System Cost Performance Database: Cost Growth Analysis Using Selected Acquisition Reports*, Santa Monica, Calif.: RAND Corporation, MR-625-OSD, 1996. Online at http://www.rand.org/pubs/monograph_reports/ MR625/ as of February 13, 2006.

Jaynes, H. R., Jr., *Correlation Analysis: Army Acquisition Program Cycle Time and Cost Variation*, unpublished masters thesis, Monterey, Calif.: Naval Postgraduate School, 1999.

Large, Joseph P., *Bias in Initial Cost Estimates: How Low Estimates Can Increase the Cost of Acquiring Weapon Systems*, Santa Monica, Calif.: RAND Corporation, R-1467-PAE, 1974. Online at http:// www.rand.org/pubs/reports/R1467/ as of February 9, 2006.

Lorell, Mark A., and John C. Graser, *An Overview of Acquisition Reform Cost Savings Estimates*, Santa Monica, Calif.: RAND Corporation, MR-1329-AF, 2001. Online at http://www.rand.org/pubs/ monograph_reports/MR1329/ as of February 8, 2006.

McNicol, D. L., *Growth in the Costs of Major Weapon Procurement Programs*, Institute for Defense Analyses, IDA Paper P-3832, 2004.

Merrow, Edward W., Kenneth Phillips, and Christopher W. Myers, *Understanding Cost Growth and Performance Shortfalls in Pioneer Process Plants*, Santa Monica, Calif.: RAND Corporation, R-2569-DOE, 1981. Online at http://www.rand.org/pubs/reports/R2569/ as of February 9, 2006.

Pfleeger, Shari Lawrence, Felicia Wu, and Rosalind Lewis, *Software Cost Estimation and Sizing Methods: Issues and Guidelines*, Santa Monica, Calif.: RAND Corporation, MG-269-AF, 2005. Online at http://www.rand.org/pubs/monographs/MG269/index.html as of February 8, 2006.

Shaw, Alan H., *Past Trends in Procurement of Air Intercept Missiles and Implications for the Advanced Medium-Range Air-to-Air Missile Program (AMRAAM)*, Congressional Budget Office Staff Working Paper, 1982. Online at http://ftp.cbo.gov/showdoc.cfm?index=5103&sequence=0 as of February 9, 2006.

Sipple, Vince, Edward White, and Michael Greiner, "Surveying Cost Growth," *Defense Acquisition Review Journal*, January–April 2004, pp. 79–91. Online at http://www.dau.mil/pubs/arq/2004arq/ White.pdf as of February 9, 2006.

Stata Corporation, *Stata Base Reference Manual*, College Station, Texas: Stata Corp., 2003, Release 8, Vol. 1, A–F.

Tyson, K. W., B. R. Harmon, and D. M. Utech, *Understanding Cost and Schedule Growth in Acquisition Programs*, Institute for Defense Analysis, IDA Paper P-2967, 1994.

Tyson, K. W., J. R. Nelson, N. I. Om, and P. R. Palmer, *Acquiring Major Systems: Cost and Schedule Trends and Acquisition Initiative Effectiveness*, Institute for Defense Analyses, IDA Paper P-2201, 1989.

Tyson, K. W., J. R. Nelson, and D. M. Utech, *A Perspective on Acquisition of NASA Space Systems*, Institute for Defense Analyses, IDA Document D-1224, 1992.

U.S. Department of Defense, Office of the Inspector General, *Acquisition: Major Defense Acquisition Programs Cost Growth*, Washington, D.C.: U.S. Department of Defense, D-2002-054, 2002. Online at http://www.dodig.osd.mil/audit/reports/fy02/02-054.pdf as of February 9, 2006.

———, Office of the Assistant Secretary of Defense (Public Affairs), "DoD Releases Selected Acquisition Reports," news release no. 795-04, August 19, 2004. Online at http://www.defenselink.mil/ releases/2004/nr20040819-1145.html as of February 8, 2006.

Wandland, K. W., and G. P. Wickman, *Analysis of Cost and Schedule Growth on Sole Source and Competitive Air Force Contracts*, unpublished masters thesis, Wright Patterson Air Force Base, Ohio: Air Force Institute of Technology, 1993.

Wolf, Jeffrey Guy, *Cost and Schedule Growth During Weapon System Acquisition: An Investigation of the Impact of Selected Economic and Political Factors*, Monterey, Calif.: Naval Postgraduate School, 1990.

Younossi, Obaid, Michael Kennedy, and John C. Graser, *Military Airframe Costs: The Effects of Advanced Materials and Manufacturing Processes*, Santa Monica, Calif.: RAND Corporation, MR-1370-AF, 2001. Online at http://www.rand.org/pubs/monograph_reports/MR1370/ as of February 8, 2006.

Younossi, Obaid, David Stem, Mark A. Lorell, and Frances M. Lussier, *Lessons Learned from the F/A-22 and F/A-18 E/F Development Programs*, Santa Monica, Calif.: RAND Corporation, MG-276-AF, 2005. Online at http://www.rand.org/pubs/monographs/MG276/index.html as of February 8, 2006.